Poems of Life

By

Lashae Phillips

Dedication

To every soul who has ever felt unseen, unheard, or unworthy—
this book is for you.

May these words wrap around your spirit like light through darkness.
May you find pieces of yourself in these poems.
And may you always remember:

You are not broken—
you are becoming.

Keep rising.
Keep healing.
Keep proving them wrong
by loving yourself right.

With all my heart

Table of Contents

The War Within

I smile in rooms where I feel alone,
        Laugh with a voice that do not sound like my own.

I carry calm, I wear control,
        But chaos screams beneath my soul.

They see a woman strong and still,
        But they do not know the strength it kills.

They see the fire in my eyes—
        They never see the quiet cries.

I battle thoughts that never sleep,
        Wounds that fester, buried deep.
        Each breath I take feels like a fight,
        Each step I take against the night.

It is not a war they would understand,
        No soldiers march, no guns in hand.
        Just shadows creeping in my chest,
        And dreams that never let me rest.

But even broken, I will not fold—
        I have made a home inside the cold.
        And though I bleed behind my grin,
        I am still surviving
        the war within.

Mass Destruction

I did not break like glass —
	I shattered like a world gone mad.
	Everything I held, everything I loved,
	Crumbled beneath a silent crash.

I warned them — do not come too near,
	My heart's a battlefield of fear.

Each smile I give is built on pain,
	Each word I speak holds acid rain.

I have loved like lightning, fierce and fast,
	But even passion does not last.

When trust is bruised and hope's undone,
	The damage cannot be outrun.

My soul is scorched, my peace is cracked,
	I carry scars that will not grow back.
	I have set fire to bridges, burned my name,
	All to survive the guilt and shame.

So, if you see me standing still,
	Know it took a storm of will.
	I am not a victim — I am the cost
	Of everything I have loved and lost.

This is not drama, this is truth,
	The kind that haunts the halls of youth.
	I am not just hurt — I am the eruption
	Of a lifetime's
	mass destruction.

A Black Businesswoman

She walks in rooms with power and grace,
    Confidence carved in every place.
    Head held high, heels sharp and tall,
    She breaks the limits, shatters the wall.

They doubted her, they told her no,
    But she just smiled and let it go.
    Built from hustle, raised by fight,
    She turned her pain into her light.

She owns her name, she owns her brand,
    No fear to speak, no need to stand.
    She moves with purpose, works with pride,

And keeps her roots deep inside.

A queen in motion, bold and wise,
    With visions stretching past the skies.
    She is not just building wealth and fame—
    She is lifting others in her name.

Cold as Ice

You thought I would melt beneath your stare,
      But I am not soft — I am built from air.
      The kind that cuts, the kind that chills,
      The kind that breaks the strongest wills.

I gave my warmth, I gave my soul,
      But now I'm done with playing roles.
      I used to beg, now I decide,
      No more tears I try to hide.

You call me bitter, call me mean,
      Just because I will not cause a scene.
      But truth be told, I paid the price—
      Now I am colder… cold as ice.

Do not take my silence for defeat,
      This frozen heart still has a beat.
      It just will not waste another day
      On someone who just walked away.

Bodyguard

You stood for me when I was weak,
       Spoke loud for me when I could not speak.
       You took the hits I could not bear,
       Fought battles just to show you care.

You did not wear a shield or sword,
       But love was sharper than a word.
       You stood like stone through every test,
       Even when your soul needed rest.

You watched the world come after me,
       Yet stayed like roots beneath a tree.
       My bodyguard, my strength, my wall—
       You never let me slip or fall.

Not just in flesh, but spirit too,
       You kept me safe and pulled me through.
       I may not say it every day,
       But I thank you in every way.

Trials and Tribulations

Life do not always go as planned,
    Sometimes it slips right through your hands.
    You fight so hard just to stay strong,
    Even when everything feels wrong.

People judge what they do not see,
    The pain behind your dignity.

You smile and nod, but deep inside,
    You carry battles you must hide.

Trials come like crashing waves,
    Testing hearts that long to be brave.
    Tribulations knock you low,
    But still you rise, and still you grow.

You cry at night, then wipe your face,
    Put on strength like it is your lace.
    Every scar becomes your crown,
    Every fall builds solid ground.

It is in the fire your soul refines,
    In broken places, healing shines.
    Though the road is rough and long,
    You are still here — and that means you are strong.

The Cries Within

I smile so bright, but deep inside,
>There is a storm I have learned to hide.
>Behind my eyes, a silent scream,
>A heart that aches, a shattered dream.

No one sees the weight I bear,
>The empty nights, the vacant stare.
>I laugh aloud, but it is a show,
>For there is a pain they will never know.

The cries within do not make a sound,
>But still, they echo all around.
>In quiet rooms and sleepless nights,
>I wrestle shadows, lose the fights.

I pray for peace, I beg for light,
>To end this long and silent fight.

Yet still, I walk, and still, I try,
>To rise again though I do not know why.

One day, the cries may find release,
>A moment of long-waited peace.
>Until that time, I wear this grin,
>And hold inside the cries within.

Stages of Life

From the cradle to the crawling floor,
    Life opens with an unseen door.
    Bright-eyed dreams and baby cries,
    A world unknown beneath blue skies.

Then come the days of scraped-up knees,
    Running wild, chasing every breeze.
    Laughter loud, and hearts so pure,
    A childhood joy we wish could endure.

Teenage years with battles inside,
    Trying to find a place to hide.

Questions big, emotions deep,
    Secrets we guard, promises we keep.

Adulthood knocks with steady pace,
    Bills and work, a faster race.
    Love is found, sometimes it fades,
    But lessons grow where truth invades.

Then middle age with wiser eyes,
    Looking back at lows and highs.
    Raising children, chasing time,
    Still trying to craft the perfect rhyme.

Old age comes with slower feet,
    But memories dance and hearts still beat.

Stories told from rocking chairs,
    Of strength, of loss, of answered prayers.

Each stage a book, a page, a rhyme,
    A ticking beat inside of time.

And when the final breath is near,
We smile back on every year.

Under the Sea

Under the sea, where the blue runs deep,
  Where secrets hide and soft waves sleep,
  A quiet world begins to glow,
  Far beneath the tide's slow flow.

The dolphins laugh, the starfish spin,
  The ocean sings from deep within.
  With every ripple, life is free,
  In the magic under the sea.

The coral blooms in colors bold,
  Like buried treasure made of gold.
  Fish in gowns of green and red
  Twirl through castles made of thread.

There's peace down here, a calming grace,
  No fear, no rush, just open space.
  A world untouched by pain or pride,
  With room for dreams the waves cannot hide.

If life above gets hard to bear,
  Close your eyes — just drift down there.
  Where hearts can float and spirits flee,
  To find their home under the sea.

Still, I Rise Inside

They tried to break me down with lies,
    But I found strength in tear-filled eyes.
    They thought I would crumble, thought I would bend,
    But pain became my oldest friend.

I have walked through fire, stood in rain,
    Learned how to smile through silent pain.
    When no one heard my inner cries,
    I wiped my face and still I rise.

They saw the scars but not the soul,
    Did not know the fight to feel whole.
    But every wound became my light,
    A mark that said, "I won the fight."

I may be quiet, may be still,
    But deep inside, I hold the will.
    To grow, to shine, to overcome—
    No matter where the hurt comes from.

So, when you see me, know this truth:
    My strength was born from lost youth.
    And though they tried, I did not hide—
    Because no matter what… I rise inside.

Can't Let Go

Can't let go of the things you did.
    Can't let go of the things you said.
    Can't let go of the memories we shared.
    Can't let go of how your love has spread.

Can't let go of your goofy smile,
    I just love to have you around.

Can't let go of the way you act.
    Can't let go of the crazy dances you did.
    Can't let go of the way you make me smile.

Can't let go of the way you think you are in charge.

Can't let go of the way you cared,
    Even when no one else was there.
    Can't let go of how you held my hand,
    And helped me through what I could not understand.

Can't let go of the look in your eyes,
    Like I was your world, your favorite prize.
    Can't let go, I have tried and tried,
    But you still live in the heart inside.

My Heart

My heart is yours,
    Your heart is mines
    Wow, it's like a great design
    Your love is silver, and my luv is gold
    It's so big that nobody can hold,
    It's just that great, but people
    Otherwise say it's fake.

Do not listen to them because they will just hate.
    The way I see it, they just want to see you break.

My heart is yours and your heart is mines
    Never in a lifetime will we break dis great design.

Through storms and trials, we still survive,
    With every beat, we feel more alive.

They can doubt us, try to tear us apart,
    But nothing can shake this faithful heart.

Even in silence, I hear your soul,
    Two hearts together, making one whole.
    This love we share is deep and true,
    Forever I'm tied in love with you.

Money

Money makes people go crazy
    In their eye's things are just blazing'
    When people see money, they just faint
    Will they ever stop to think—

Money, money, money...

Money is like a powerful thing
    Things like that will never make me go insane
    Open your eyes, feel the pain, relax your brain
    Money shall never make people feel the pain or go insane.

It's not the bills that break your soul,
    It is the greed that swallows you whole.
    Chasing wealth, we lose our way,
    Forgetting peace in the light of day.

Some use it just to feel strong,
    But power built on cash will not last long.
    It fades like smoke, it leaves like rain,
    And all you are left with is the stain.

Why not trade the gold for grace?
    Kindness leaves a better trace.
    Rich in heart is wealth that stays,
    And lights your path through darkest days.

Endless Love

Endless love is what I want
        Endless love is what I need
        Do you have that love?

Just tell me, please.

This love is hard to find
        You will never see it on an arrow pointing to a line
        Yes, love like this is fine.

It is not made of perfect words or gold,
        But stories shared and hands we hold.
        It is in the way you stay through storms,
        And how you cherish every form.

Endless love will not fade with time,
        It lives in rhythm, heart, and rhyme.
        So if you got it, do not let go—
        It's rarer than the world will show.

What I Think

Letting your guard down to
        someone special is a warm and
        embarrassing thing because you feel
        comfortable around that person.

If you feel like you are safe around
        the person and they always keep
        you are smiling, then it is a wonderful
        thing. Most people feel like
        they will never find that special
        woman or man because they think
        there is no such thing as true love.

Well, I say people need to just
        let go of all their worries and
        let God take care of them. They
        just need to wait, and they will
        see God has something good planned
        for them.

People should be
        thinking about how blessed they
        are because some people could not
        see another day and be with
        their family.

Sometimes love takes time to grow,
        Like flowers blooming slow.
        But trust in what the heart can feel—
        What is meant for you will be real.

So, take a breath and hold on tight,
        Through every dark, await the light.

There's joy ahead you cannot see,
A life of hope and destiny.

Is it True?

Is it true that he is the love
        Of my life???
        Is it true it was love at first
        Sight,

What would I do if he were gone
        In a blink of an eye,
        Maybe I would sit down and
        Cry or just wonder why.

Is it true I would spend the
        Rest of my life with him or
        Would I go off on my own and
        Make things be known.

Will I be the next African American
        To make a difference in life.
        And is it true that I am
        Blinded by love. Is it true I
        Cannot see the main man above.

Is it true he will never break
        My heart and make sure
        Nothing will fall apart or is
        He is filling my head up with crazy
        Things and making them into
        A big dream.

Or is it all just in my mind—
        Wishing for a love that's kind,
        Hoping he is the one for real
        But not sure how I should feel.

Is it true this love is fate,
      Or am I walking through a gate
      To something I do not really see—
      Just chasing what was never meant to be.

Why?

Why is it that you still
        In my head. Is it because
        Of the things you did or is
        It because you are the one
        I really love. I really do not
        Know, but a part of me is
        Saying stays and another part
        Is saying just go. I am so
        Confused I do not know what
        To do.

Is it because of you.
        I just need to know
        The truth. Wishing it could
        Go away but instead it is
        Just building up in my head.

Why does my heart replay
        Every word you used to say?
        Moments echo loud and clear,
        Even when you are not nearby.

Is it hope or just the fear
        Of losing what I held so dear?
        Your shadow lingers like a thread,
        Tangled deep inside my head.

Never Gone Change

It has never gone change between us.
        I still love him, and he still loves me.
        One day, we will get back together,
        because it has never gone change.

The things we been through is
        not worth throwing all away.
        It has never gone change.
        We had that crazy love, that
        love that had an effect on
        other people. I will always
        love him and care for him
        because it has never gone change.

We gave up too easily. We are so
        stubborn and we have that
        I do not care attitude. Our love
        is too strong to let go.
        It has never gone change.

I still replay our laughs in my mind,
        Even on days when you are not kind.
        I act like I am fine, but deep down I ache,
        Because losing you felt like my biggest mistake.

I cry in silence, hold in the pain,
        Still checking my phone, hoping you feel the same.

I miss your voice, even when it shook,
        I'd take the fights if I could get back the look—
        the way you looked at me like I was the one.
        Now that gaze is gone, but my heart is not done.

We both messed up, yes, that is true,
But do not act like you did not love me too.
Our love was fire, loud and real,
Now I am left with scars I still got to feel. Say what you want, play
your little game but you and me? We never gone change.

What Is Love

Love is a powerful word.
    Love is a word that makes someone feel special.
    Love is a word that has been abused so many times.
    Love is just another four-letter word that nobody takes seriously.
    It is a word that you must show and mean.

Love means you have strong feelings for someone,
    But it also means that that person means the world to you.
    Love is something you should show.

Love is patient when the world moves fast,
    It is holding on tight when nothing seems to last.
    Love is messy, it can break you down,
    But it is the same thing that can turn life around.

Love is late-night talks and unspoken fears,
    It is wiping away someone else's tears.
    Love is truth, even when it is hard to say,
    It is showing up for someone every single day.

It Hurts

It hurts when the one you love betrays you.
    It hurts when they say the words,

"I'm not in love with you."
    It hurts when they leave you in the dark to suffer in pain,
    And now you have no more tears left to drain.

It hurts when your heart has been broken into two,
    And you are just sitting there, saying
    What am I going to do.

It hurts when memories will not let you sleep,
    When silence gets loud, and the wounds cut deep.

It hurts when your smile becomes a disguise,
    And you fake being strong while you are dying inside.

Do not Give Up

Do not give up on the person you love.
    Do not say what you cannot do,
    Look at friends and tell them
    You believe in them too.

Do not put someone down.
    Do not tell a child they will not be nothing.
    Do not go to school and act out.
    Do not roam the streets all the time.
    Do not join gangs and get yourself killed.

Do not smoke your money away and then you cannot pay your bill.

Do not take advantage of good people.
    Do not hold grudges against your friends and family.

Do not quit just because it is hard—
    Diamonds form under pressure, not in the yard.

Do not break down when life do not play fair,
    Stand up, speak truth, show that you care.

Do not forget that pain means you are still alive,
    It means you are still fighting, still trying to survive.

Do not let the streets write your fate,
    There is more to life—you are not too late.

Do not ignore your worth, your power inside,
    Even broken wings find ways to glide.

Sweet Honesty

Sweet honesty is like a bowl of honey,
    But everybody just want money.
    Why isn't it the most popular thing?
    Maybe because people can buy bling.

Things just get so crazy, it makes you go insane.

Life filled with wonderful things,
    You do not know what comedy brings.
    Enjoy your days while you can
    Because you will never know when you stand your last stand.

Live your life to the fullest,
    It is your last day to live and your dreams you may fulfill

Be real even when it is hard to be,
    Truth shines brighter than what people see.

Do not let the fake tear your spirit apart,
    Speak your truth straight from the heart.

And when the world starts turning cold,
    Let sweet honesty be the gold you hold.

Can We Be

Can we be more than just friends.
 Can we be like the days that never end.
 Can we be like the sun & clouds in
 the sky rising above every living guy.

Can we be the blood that flows to the heart.
 Can we be the ones that made a fresh start.
 Can we be the two who make millions.
 Can we be the fruit that keeps everyone healthy.

Can we be the ones to show everybody how to love again?

Can we be the ones who help others out.
 Can we be the ones to show them what it's all about.
 Can we be the ones who show people how to be romantic.
 Can we be the two people to tell others not to be drastic.

Can we be the rhythm in a world off beat,
 The calm in chaos, the peace on the street.

Can we be the dream no one thought was real,
 The love that heals what they thought would not heal.

I Wish

I wish I could hear you say, "Honey, I'm home."
    I wish we could have done things different.
    I wish we never broke up the first time.
    I wish I could still say you is my husband
    when they say, "Hey Ms. Watson."

I wish that my love for you will never fade,
    so bad that it cannot be seen.

When I wake up every morning'
    I wish I could kiss and hug you a thousand times.
    I wish this night was a night I could get on a heart boat—
    when you said the words, "I'm your #1 girl,"
    I wish that it stays true.

I wish I could wake up next to you,
    seeing' you smile and look into your eyes.
    I wish I could be the one who cooks your dinner
    when you come home from a long day at work.

I wish I can be the one who takes care of you
    when you are sick.

Growing old together as grandparents
    is what I wish for.

I wish we could have had a family of our own.
    I wish, I wish, I wish…
    I wish I could just hug and kiss you this one last time.

I wish I could rewind time and fix the cracks.
    Turn pain into laughter, bring those moments back.
    I wish you knew I still talk to the moon,
    hoping' my whispers will reach you soon.

I wish I could lay your favorite shirt on my chest,
    feel your scent and just rest.

I wish I weren't still dreaming of you at night,
    but it is the only place we still feel right in.

I wish you would knock on that door out the blue,
    saying,' "I still love you too." But until then, I will keep wishing.

holding on to the love that is missing.

A Good Woman

Someone I love so much is too hurt.
      Just tell me, will things ever work?
      I love to see him smile, but
      Never will I love to see him down.

Making him happy and giving him the world,
      It is like a great big joy cuts apart of my world.

Taking care of him when he is sick,
      Loving him through thick n thin,
      Helping him get through his trials n tribulations,
      Is a vow I am willing to take.

I will pray for him when he cannot find the words,
      Stand strong for him when life seems blurred.

Even when he is tired, broken, or lost,
      I will love him deeper—no matter what the cost.

I will not walk away when the nights get cold,
      I will be his shelter, steady and bold.

Not just a lover, but his peace and his friend,
      A good woman holds on, right till the end.

So even when the world does not understand,
      I'll still be here, holding' his hand.
      Not for praise, not for show—
      But because real love does not let go.

True Love

True love is what we have.
	Never shall I take a chance or not tell.
	I love you and you love me—
	yes... our love shall last eternally.
	Why do they hate on our love?
	Because we… the best.

Yes, our love does affect.
	True love is what we have.

Even in the dark, your light still shines,
	A bond so real, it breaks all lines.
	They talk, they whisper, they throw shade,
	But what we got? It will never fade.

You hold my heart without a doubt,
	Through storms and pain, we tough it out.
	I ride for you, and you ride for me,
	That's how real loves supposed to be.

When the world cold and full of lies,
	We look at each other with open eyes.

They don't get it, they never will—
	What we feel is raw, it is deep, it is real.

So let them talk, let them stare,
	True love like this is so rare.
	You my peace, you my flame,
	And I will never let them shame our name.

Missing You

I'll be missing you when u leave.
       I know at times it will feel like I can't breathe.
       Goin back down memory lane
       will make me feel so much pain.
       Seeing u smile or getting your hugs
       is something I won't have or see every day.
       But while you're gone, God will make a way.

Missing You.

Not hearing your voice say "I LOVE YOU"
       will make me die slowly inside.
       I know u will always be right by my side.
       Us giving up is something we won't be doing.
       Makin our love grow is what we will be improving.

Nights get cold and the tears will fall,
       I will whisper to the stars, hoping you hear it all.
       Your scent still lingers in the air,
       I reach out at night, wishing you were there.

My pillow's soaked, my heart feels tight,
       Missing you hard every single night.
       But even in pain, I still believe—
       You will come back and never leave.

Prove It

You say you will be the best you can be...
    Prove it.
    You say you will graduate...
    Prove it.
    When people said all the hurtful things about you,
    You said you would become the opposite of everything they said
    you wouldn't be...
    Prove it.
    You said you will make a change...
    Prove it.
    You said you can make something of yourself...
    Prove it.
    You said you can, and you will make your dream come true...
    Prove it.

They say success is far away,
    But you're walking toward it every day...
    Prove it.
    They say you'll fall just like the rest,
    But you're pushing through every test...
    Prove it.
    They said your past would define who you are,
    But you've already come so far...
    Prove it.

Let your scars be your story,
    Turn your pain into glory...
    Prove it.
    Even when they doubt your light,
    Shine with everything in sight...
    Prove it.
    You've got the fire, the fight, the drive—

You were born to rise and thrive...
Prove it.

He's Running Game

He says all the right things, does all the right things—
    But when will I ever see them truly emerge?
    My body's here, my heart is near,
    But he doesn't even seem to care.
    He made that real clear.
    He's running game.

Hours and hours pass me by,
    And still, I sit and wonder why.
    Tears fall, but I fight to stay sane,
    Trying hard to numb this pain.

Being happy is what I need,
    So I will not let him make me bleed.
    He is pulling me apart—piece by piece,
    But I swear I will find my peace.
    He is running game.

Excuses stacked on top of lies,
    A thousand truths he tries to disguise.
    It is time I see him for who he is—
    He is not the man I thought he was.

It is time to make a change.
    This love is twisted, strange.
    It is driving me insane,
    And I am done playing his game.

I would have never caused him pain,
    But he left me standing in the rain.
    Now I rise and walk away—
    I am choosing me, starting today.

Shocking News

On a hot sunny day, we got the
        most shocking news. When we heard
        the news, it was like singing the blues.
        Nobody ever thought something like this
        would ever come or happen,
        Hearts beating fast and racing like
        they on a racetrack. Family wishing
        they could all just go back.
        Tears falling like rain drops, hoping
        that the pain stops. He left us
        all wondering why. Because we
        really were not ready for him to die.

Nobody ever knew his pain. He only
        took it for so long that it made him
        go insane. He must have said to himself "Why
        not take my life away" and never
        again will I have to see another day.

And now we sit, staring at the wall,
        Waiting for his name to call.
        But silence hits harder than sound,
        Because he is no longer around.

His smile still stuck in my head,
        Cannot believe that he is dead.
        He wore his pain just like a mask,
        Now peace is all we ask.

So, check on your strong friends, please,
        They hide the hurt with too much ease.

The ones who laugh the loudest cries—
        They fight the hardest not to die.

A Reminder from Me to You

Stay strong, my love—your storm will cease,
    The winds will calm, your soul finds peace.
    God's got your back, do not you forget,
    You are here for purpose, not regret.

You are not a flaw, you are heaven-sent,
    Each tear you have cried, each moment spent
    Was never wasted—not in vain,
    God walks beside you through the rain.

There are still hearts who love you true,
    Though doubt may cloud your point of view.
    You are needed here, do not ever stray—
    God made you special in His way.

He sees your strength, He knows your fire,
    He lifts you when the path climbs higher.

Ignore the ones who speak in spite,
    Just smile and shine your inner light.

When hate or lies come into view,
    Say, "God bless you, and I love you too."
    They may not get you—give it time,
    The truth will ring, just like a chime.

So, hold your faith—do not let it fade,
    You are like a star that God has made.
    Let no one dim your glowing flame,
    You are more than strong—you will rise again.

You got this, my little star!

Be blessed.
    Stay blessed.

And always...
Be a blessing.

Just Like Plastic

I was thinking he was real.
     All the love he showed, it did appeal—
     But come to find out, he isn't nun but plastic.
     If a nigga tells you he loves you,
     Just look at him and say,
     "I love me too."

Everything that glitters is not gold.
     He is just like plastic.
     Sometimes it might hurt your soul.

When someone ask you,
     Do they have anything to worry about—
     Every time you turn around,
     Then something is not right.

Just make sure you have the sight to see,
     Because you are blinded by love.
     But just know you will always have the man above.

He is just like plastic.

You gave your all, your time, your trust,
     But he turned your diamonds back into dust.
     Told you lies so sweet, now they taste bitter—
     The truth hit hard, but your souls much bigger.

So, hold your head and let him go,
     He is not the love you are meant to know.
     The pain will pass, the real will last—
     He was just plastic, part of the past.

How Much Love

He's the love of my life
    My love for him is so high
    It is like a diamond in the sky
    When he is hurt, I just cry
    My love for him is so strong
    I will never want to see him gone.

My love for him is so high
    It is like a kite flying high
    He is the love of my life; never ever
    Will I stab him with a knife
    If he says the words Bye-Bye
    I will just fall and cry.

My heart will drop into a box like
    A mouse got caught by a fox.

My love for him is so high, it seems
    Like I will never die.

When he is near, my heart races.

A million thoughts, a million faces

I will hold him close, never let go

Even if the world tells me no.

Another One Gone

Coming home from a good day of
      school not worrying' about anything...
      As I came through the door I
      heard seven words —
      "They found your uncle dead in his house."

When I heard that I was shocked.
      But the only thing I could say in my
      head was, "Another one gone."

We all wonder why it happen
      so fast, and what was the
      cause. I do not think anything was
      ever solved.

Everybody thought about all
      the good things that happened in the past,
      knowing that all the memories would last.

We sit around talking,' laughing',
      actin' like everything okay,
      but deep down we feel that pain
      every single day.

Another life gone, another tear
      we try to hide.
      We still feel that empty space
      we carry deep inside.

A picture, a laugh, a story told—
      they come back when the nights get cold.
      And even though you are gone from sight,
      you live in our hearts every night.

Tell Me Why

Tell me why do we have to
     act our color?

Tell me why we do not get along.

Tell me why we fight, shoot,
     and kill one another.

Tell me why we make a big
     deal out of nothing.

Tell me why we do scandalous
     things.

Tell me why we do not act like
     good human beings.

Tell me why we hurt the
     people we love.

Tell me why we do not go
     to the man above.

Tell me why we do not get a good education
     while we can.

Tell me why we abandon the ones who
     trust in us.

Tell me why we are always saying what
     we cannot do and never what we can do.

Do We Mean It

Do we mean it when we say
    the words "I hate you?

Do we mean it when we do
    cold-hearted things?

Do we mean it when we tell
    someone they will never grow
    to be someone in life?

Do we mean it when we say,
    I hope you go away and never come back?

Do we mean it when we call
    our kids out, they name,
    everything but the child of God?

Do we mean it when we are saying
    I will make you suffer
    like you made them suffer?

Do we mean it when we do
    downlow things to hurt our loved ones?

Do we mean it
    when we walk away in silence,
    knowing we broke somebody
    who would have stayed?

Do we mean it
    when we turn love into war,
    peace into pain,
    just to feel powerful again?

Do we mean it?

Love Hard

We love so hard that we know
    Cannot nothing fall apart.
    Even though we hurt so bad, deep down inside
    We still love hard.

We give our all
    But yet at the end,
    We still gone fall.
    We love them like it is the end of the world.

Things spin and things twirl.

We cry at night
    But still answer the phone like we are all right.
    We hold it in,
    Keep smiling
    Even when we done fighting.

They don't even see the pain we hide,
    We just ride and ride,
    Till our hearts cannot take no more—
    But we stay,
    Because that is what loving hard is for.

We bend,
    We break,
    But still choose them
    Like its fate.

A Special Day

Picking a month and a day out of a year is a special day.
        When your soulmate gets down on one knee and says the words.

WILL YOU MARRY ME?! That is your special day.

Being able to get up in the morning,
        Not having to cook or clean
        Because the man of your dreams has come into your life—
        That is a good thing.

But now… your time has come.

On July 10th, 2010,
        A very special day,
        Because you get to say the words.

I DO.

After saying I DO,
        You have closed your doors to your past
        And opened new doors
        To someone special.

Death

Death is a scary thing
        The way people die, it should not be seen
        Bodies dropping on streets with no name
        And all we do is replay the blame.

Things are done so strange
        People numb like it's normal, but it is deranged.
        Mama's cry while babies bleed
        But change will not come if we don't lead.

People should want to change,
        We living in pain that feels prearranged.
        Another candlelight, another name on a shirt
        How many got to go before we feel the hurt?

Everyday people get shot and killed
        No reason, just anger that never got healed.
        Some die by stray bullets, some by hate
        And all we do is say "It's just fate."

Never shall we watch things like that spill
        Like blood in the gutter do not give us chills.
        We supposed to rise, not fall deeper
        But this world keeps getting colder, not sweeter.

We should use our skills to do good things
        Build each other up, give each other wings.
        Not go around and kill every human being
        Like life do not matter, like we aren't seeing.

Death is a scary thing—
        Not just the end, but the silence it brings.
        The kind that makes you question why
        So many must suffer, so many must die.

I'll Be There

I'll be there when you go through hard times
        Never will I leave you in a lonely dime.
        I'll be right by your side
        Even when the ground of the earth opens wide.

When the ocean tides rise,
        There you will see, my love will abide.
        My love for you is so high,
        It's just like a hurricane reaching up toward the sky.
        If I die before I wake,
        My love for you I shall take.

I'll be there when the nights feel too long,
        When you cry in the dark and feel like you don't belong.
        I won't turn my back when you're broken inside,
        I'll sit in the silence with you, I won't hide.

When the world gets too heavy for your hands to hold,
        When your heart turns cold and your soul feels old,
        I'll be the warmth in your storm, the peace in your fight,
        The voice that reminds you, you gone' be alright.

Even if the rain pours harder than pain,
        Even if you lose yourself again and again,
        I will be there through every test and tear,
        Not just in words—I will really be nearby.

My love is not temporary, it is built to stay,
        Like roots in the ground that do not blow away.
        I will be there when hope feels like it is gone,
        Still holding' you down, still singing' your song.

So, if I go before the morning comes,
        If breath leaves me and my heart stops drumming',

Just know, even in heaven's space,
My love for you still got a place.

What If

What if I told you I love you
    What if I said I hate you
    What if I wanted to be with you
    What if I said I want to leave you

What if
    What if I packed my bags without saying good-bye???
    Would you hate me for the rest of your life
    What if I change my mind and say, "baby be mine"
    Would you love me 'til I die?

What if I cried behind closed doors,
    Wrote your name on fogged-up mirrors
    And whispered your name into pillows
    That don't hold your shape anymore?

What if I stayed up at night
    Wondering if you ever think of me—
    If my silence ever screams
    Louder than my words did?

What if I left because I was scared
    Of loving too hard,
    Of being loved too soft,
    Of not being enough?

What if I came back,
    Different, broken, but brave enough to try again—
    Would you hold out your arms,
    Or hold onto your pride?

What if we were never meant to last
    But always meant to matter?

Would you still remember me
    When the world forgets our names?

What if the only time you see me again
    Is in the middle of a dream—
    Would you wake up missing me,
    Or grateful I am finally gone? Just what if the love we buried
    Was the only real thing
    We ever had

The Love I Once Had

The love once had for you
	Was not ordinary—
	It was deep,
	Deeper than the darkest parts
	Of the deep blue sea.

You touched places
	No one ever reached—
	With just your smile,
	You reached a kind of peace
	I did not know I needed.

It was hard to let you go.
	My heart screamed NO,

The days roll by—
	Memories fade,
	But not the heart ache and pain

I miss you in the quiet and in the spaces between breaths.

I miss you like summer misses spring
	When the winter comes too fast.

And when you walked away,
	You did not just leave but you took pieces.

Now I am left with shadows and echoes,
	Tracing where your love used to live.

They say time heals,
	But all it has done was remind me.

The love I once had for you was the kind that made my heart soar—
	it was not just real.

It was forever.
Even if you were not.

How I Love Him

I think he is the one—
        Yes, he is the one, my only one.
        I just know he is the one.

I love him like I love my mama,
        I love him like they love Obama.

I love him like I love my daddy—
        It would not matter if they said,
        "Look at that big fatty."

I love him like I love my sisters,
        I would not care if he played hooky
        He has my heart,
        I have his heart.
        If this love does not last,
        I know for a fact—
        that time has passed.

More Than Friends

You start off as friends,
    but while you tell each other your problems,
    you become more than friends.

When you are going through things
    and get emotional,
    your friend will be right there helping you.

But as you look around,
    you will finally see
    that you have become more than friends.

If you are in a relationship with someone
    and you want to spend the rest of your life with them,
    but you start to feel a connection
    between you and your friend—
    then it means you are becoming
    more than friends.

A Great Man

A great man is a man who can
        bring you out of all your trials and tribulations.
        A great man can help every homeless person on this world
        and make sure they have food to eat.

Do you know who this great man is?

A great man is a savior who will
        protect you from any harm that comes your way.

A great man is a man who will forgive you
        for all the wrong you have done
        and will answer all your prayers at any time.

A great man will show and make a way.
        This great man is our one and only
        Heavenly Father.

Fire

The fire in my veins
        is raging.
        The hatred in my heart
        is rising.
        You shut me out without a doubt,
        Wondering to myself—
        What is that all about?

Standing in the dark all alone,
        Waiting to see—
        Will you come home?

The silence burns louder than screams,
        Echoing through my shattered dreams.

Your absence strikes like a heavy flame,
        And nothing around me feels the same.

I pace these halls of memory and smoke,
        Clutching words we never spoke.

Your ghost still lingers in the air,
        A presence, cold, that is not fair.

You built a wall I cannot climb,
        Left me frozen in stolen time.
        But still, I wait beside the ash,
        Longing for a spark to flash.

If love once lived in what we knew,
        Can fire cleanse and carry through?
        Or will I stand and burn in vain,
        Caught between love, anger, and pain?

Making It

Making it through life is hard.
    Hoping your friends and loved ones stay by your side.
    Everything will just fall apart,
    Taking it step by step and day by day.
    Just maybe things won't fade away.
    Wishing, hoping you could see another day.

Making it

Just live off the real.
    God will show you a way out to the light.
    The one you love will always be there,
    No matter what.
    If something goes wrong, just go to God for help,
    And he will—
    And I mean, he will make a way.

Just know that you are blessed,
    And the great man above
    Has something good planned for you
    Later on in life.

Just For You

Ashes to ashes,
        Dust to dust,
        But it is you whom
        I should have trust.

The connection is too
        Strong to forgive and forget.
        The love I have for you—
        I cannot neglect.

To watch you finally walk away
        Is something that I never thought
        I would see you do forever in a day.

As the tears rolled down my face,
        I tried to forget the moments I retraced.

Always thinking about your kiss
        And your warm embrace,
        But it will never be replaced.

Love

Love is like a roller coaster—
    It goes up and it goes down.
    Sometimes it will go all the way around.

If you feel like I feel,
    You will never have a frown.

Sometimes I may be down,
    But the good love in you will never stay down.

I see you; you see me—
    Together we leave town.

Love is a powerful word
    That goes up and down.

Remember, remember, remember:
    Love is like a roller coaster.
    It goes up & it goes down,
    And sometimes it will go all the way around.

God's Child

Trying to get through this storm to see the sunshine.
    Everything that I touch will be mine.
    How do I know? Because God gave me a sign.

I may stumble and I may fall,
    But I will get back up and surely stand tall.

I am God's child! Why?
    Because no matter what I go through,
    I will always smile and refuse to stay down.

With the strength in my body and the love in my heart,
    Any child of the devil will never break me apart.
    So move around because I'm coming through.

I'll stop and say hello and goodbye to you.

You may hate me, but I love you.
    You may do me wrong,
    But I'll stay true.

Even when you fall, I will pick you up. Why?
    Because I will surely stand tall!

My heart is filled with love
    All because of the man above.

People wonder why I stay on top.
    It is because that man above is my rock.

So, if you like what you see,
    Join the team—because the blessings never stop.
    I look to the left, I look to the right,
    Everything I see is a beautiful sight.

Yes!! God has a plan,
    That is why I continue to stand.

That evil thang downstairs is ready to see me fall,
    But I am God's child,
    Standing tall with my head up high. I am ready for war,
    And I will fight like never before.
    What's war without a fight?
    As His child, my light will shine bright.

Devastating Call

72

Sitting around waiting on information,
    Family looking sad, it isn't anything like visitation.
    She said the words "bye-bye,"
    Like it is her last day being in the world,
    Knowing she has seen the light, bright as a pearl.

Couldn't stand the way she acted or her ways,
    But the whole time she
    Was getting us ready for the rough days.
    She loved us dearly, and yes, she made it clear—
    Family in the waiting room, scared to death,
    Crying their eyes out.

All hoping she would make it out,
    Sitting at home waiting on the phone to ring,
    Wishing the doctor can tell us something.

When they finally called,
    It was a call we all did not want.
    It was the devastating call.
    We heard the words:
    "Sorry, she just passed."

I cried, they cried, we all cried.
    I cried tears like a waterfall,
    Knowing things won't be the same at all.

We still love her with all our hearts.
    That day, everything fell apart.
    So many souls have been lost.
    It felt like our hearts were
    Ripped out and tossed.

My Lost

Ever since I lost my baby,
      things haven't been the same.
      It seems like I'm quietly going insane.
      Somebody please tells me why this happens to me.
      I know I should give it a rest,
      but I just can't let this be.

My heart is filled with anger and pain,
      and my temper has gotten worse,
      and it's a shame.
      Some days I don't want to get out the bed,
      I just want to stay home instead.
      I'm happy one minute
      and mad the next minute.

It has been seven months
      and I am still dealing with it.
      I know everything happens for a reason,
      but I still cannot believe it.

I keep a smile on my face
      so that people will not see I am in a bad place.
      I stay low key so I can be at peace,
      but at the same time,
      I know it is not good for me.

I Cry for the Little Girl That's Inside

I cry for the little girl that is inside,
        the one who cannot let go of her pride.
        She tries her best every day,
        praying' and hoping' her problems will fade away.

Nobody understands what she is going' through,
        but if she's got God,
        she knows she will pull through. I cry for the little girl that's inside,
        she is trying' to clear her mind
        as time passes by.

It is sad to say
        that everything is eating her up inside—
        all because nobody is by her side. I cry for the little girl that's
        inside,
        who never had her dad
        by her side.

That little girl may stumble and fall,
        but she will lift her head up
        and stand tall.
        Because at the end of the day,
        her goals are to reach for it all.

I cry for the little girl
        who smiles when she is hurt,
        who laughs just to cover the dirt.

She acts like she good,
        but deep down she is not,
        trying to survive every storm she got.

She does not ask for much,
        just peace and truth,

but the world keep knocking'
the light out her youth.
Still—
she doesn't fold, she does not quit,
she got that fire, and she lives with it.

I cry for the little girl because she is broken but is not weak.
	She is going to rewrite her story
	every time she speaks.

Who Am I

I am the girl you wish you had.
 I am the girl you could make your wife.
 I am the girl that makes you happy,
 The one you want to keep in your life.

Who am I?

I am the girl that catches your eye,
 The one that makes you wonder why.
 I am the one who won't lie to you,
 I am the one who will love you true.

Who am I?

I am the one who will stay by your side,
 Hold you down 'til the day you die.
 I am the one who helps you breathe
 When you feel like you cannot even believe.

Who am I?

I am your one-and-only,
 The love of your life.
 The one you cannot live without,
 Not for any price.

So, ask yourself again—

Who am I?

A Touch of Soul

It does not take much —
        just a touch of soul.
        Not loud, not flashy,
        just quiet and bold.

It's the way you move
        when the world feel heavy,
        the way you love
        when your heart is not ready.

It is the pain you hide
        behind your smile,
        but still show up
        and walk that mile.

It is eyes that seen
        too much too soon,
        but still dream big
        under a cracked-up moon.

It is holding' on
        when you want to let go,
        and speaking' truth
        even when they say no.

A touch of soul —
        it is in your hands,
        how you lift the broken
        and still take a stand.

It is in the music
        you cry to at night,
        in the words you write
        when you are tired of the fight.

It is in that old church song
        your grandma would hum,
        and the feeling' you get
        when your past come undone.

It is not about status,
        money or gold real value lives
        in a touch of soul.

Suspense

I feel it in my chest —
	heartbeat skipping
	like a warning in the dark
	that something is missing.

Shadows moving
	where they should not be,
	whispers louder
	than what eyes can see.

It is the silence
	that speaks the loudest,
	the chill in the room
	when it's feeling the proudest.

Eyes over shoulders,
	doors slightly cracked,
	I swear I saw something'
	but I am not looking back.

Tension thick
	like heavy smoke,
	every breath I take
	feels like I might choke.

My thoughts race
	but I do not run, I just stand still and wait for what's to come.

The unknown creeps
	with no footsteps heard,
	you feel it more
	than you see a word.

Maybe it is fear, maybe it's truth, a moment that shakes the core of your
	youth.

It is not always a scream,
	sometimes it is a stare,
	a sudden cold breeze
	that is not even there.

Goosebumps rise,
	sweat hits your skin, and you do not know
	where this story begins.

Love & Flowers

Love is not always soft —
    but it can be.
    Like flowers growing'
    from broken concrete.

It does not always come
    wrapped in roses,
    sometimes it is thorns
    and hearts that close in.

But when it is real,
    you feel it deep.

Like petals falling'
    while the worlds asleep.

It is laughing' on bad days,
    crying' on good ones.
    It is holding' each other
    when the pain still runs.

Love is messy,
    like dirt on your hands
    after planting' seeds
    you hope will stand.

But when it blooms —
    it is worth the wait.

Like wildflowers
    growing' past the gate.

It does not need fancy,
    do not need show.

Just water it right
and let it grow.

So, if you love me,
    love me true —
    do not pick my petals,
    help me bloom too.

I Come from Greatness

I come from chains,
        but I also come from crowns.
        From fields of cotton
        to shutting' systems down.

I come from Malcolm, who spoke with fire.

From Rosa,
        who sat and sparked desire.

I come from Harriet,
        who ran with no fear.
        From the Underground whispers we still hear.

I come from Martin,
        with a dream so bold,
        and from Black mothers
        whose stories has not been told.

I come from fists raised,
        from blood on streets,
        from protest signs and tired feet.

I come from soul food,
        from gospel and blues,
        from Black skin magic
        they try to use.

I come from kings
        that history erased,
        and queens who ruled
        with poise and grace.

They want our rhythm,
        but not our truth tries to dim the fire

in our youth. But I walk with giant in my bloodline.
When I speak, I speak all the time.

So do not tell me I am not enough. I am built from legends,
I am made tough. This Black skin
is not just skin —
It is history,
it is fight,
it is where I begin.

Heartbreak

Heartbreak do not knock it just shows up.
        Do not care if you ready,
        do not care if you are tough.

You gave your heart, kept it real,
        Calls get short,
        vibes feel strange.

You stay up late
        with a pillow full of tears,
        thinking' 'bout all
        y'all built for years.

You scroll through pics, read old texts, trying to figure out what where it
        left.

You blame yourself,
        you reply with the signs,
        wish you could go back
        and press rewind.
        Tryna smile in public,
        but inside, it is worse.

You feel played,
        feel used, feel small.
        But deep down,
        you still stand tall.

Yes, heartbreak heavy,
        but you gone survive
        but you will come back alive.

One day you will love again,
        but smarter this time.

No more falling' for lies,
    no more wasting' your prime.

So, cry if you need to,
    scream if you must —
    but do not stay broken,
    get back up — trust.

I Have a Dream Like Martin L. King

I got a dream,
        like Martin L. King.
        A dream so deep,
        it makes my spirit sing. The things we do
        got to be seen —
        we are living life,
        but we are chasing dreams.

Dreams aren't just for sleeping',
        they are special, they are real.
        If we change this world,
        we can start to heal.

It could be beautiful,
        if we just believe,
        but first we got to give,
        not just receive.

I got a dream
        where we all rise,
        where love wins out
        and hate just dies.

With dreams,
        you can go far —
        from pain and struggle,
        to shine like stars.

Good things happen
        when your hearts in the fight.
        Keep your vision strong,
        keep your soul in the light.

We should be like Martin,
        stand tall, speak true.
        Make a difference —
        do what we were born to do.

Change the world,
        change the game.
        Stand proud and say,
        "I got a dream" —

Make A Change

Martin Luther King, Rosa Parks,
        Harriet Tubman — they lit the spark.
        They did not wait, did not stay in their lane,
        They stood up strong and made a change.

So why not us? What is holding us back?
        We got talent, strength — we do not lack.
        We got voices that rise, truth that burns,
        It is our time now, it is our turn.

Let us stand tall, speak loud and clear,
        Let them know we will not live in fear.
        We will rise above the hate and pain,
        Break the silence, break the chain.

Let those hateful words just fly,
        Like birds drifting across the sky.
        We are not bound by yesterday —
        We build tomorrow, starting today.

In this generation, we will lead,
        Plant the truth, grow the seed.
        No more waiting, no delay —
        We rise united, no matter what happens.

We can,
        we must,
        and we will
        be heard.

Black on Black Crime

We commit Black-on-Black crime,
>Then act surprised when we are doing time.
>Somebody tell me — who is going to say,
>"That's okay," and look the other way?

Babies raising babies,
>Seasons shifting — no real winters lately.

Better open your eyes and see,
>God is speaking, sending signs clearly.

What is going on with this generation?
>Nobody stands for true foundation.
>Have we ever come together and tried to say,
>"We got each other — come what may?"

Correct me if I am wrong,
>But when God removes what you lean on,
>You find out quick you are not that strong.

The things we do, the things we say,
>Lead to cuffs and time locked away.

But if you can calm the rage inside,
>And let your pride be cast aside —
>God will shield you from the strife,
>Because He is the One who gives new life.

Unfold Me

Unfold me—
        not like a letter meant to be read once
        and thrown into a drawer,
        but like a map of somewhere
        you never knew existed
        until your soul got lost
        and needed a way back.

I am not polished.
        I am not pretty lines in a perfect box.
        I am scribbles and second guesses,
        a mouth full of truth
        that does not always land soft.

They want clean edges—
        I bleed ink instead.
        I wear my hurt on my hands
        and my hope in my mouth,
        spitting dreams
        even when the world chokes back.

You think I am fragile,
        but I've broken and built myself more times
        than I can count.
        That's not weakness—
        that's survival. I do not ask to be saved. I ask to be seen.
        And if you are looking, really looking, you will find beauty
        in every scar
        I never hid.

Lashae Phillips is a bold and authentic voice in contemporary poetry, known for expressing raw emotion and real-life experiences through rhythmic storytelling. Born with a natural gift for words, she began writing to process the world around her, turning her struggles, observations, and personal growth into heartfelt verses that resonate with readers from all walks of life.

Raised in an environment that taught her strength and independence, Lashae found solace in writing early on. What began as journal entries and poems scribbled in notebooks eventually blossomed into a powerful creative outlet. Her poetry captures the highs and lows of life—love, friendship, pain, healing, self-worth, and survival—with honesty and a touch of humor.

Poems of Life is her debut collection, a testament to her journey as a woman, a fighter, a friend, and a truth-teller. Each poem invites readers into her world, offering both vulnerability and resilience. Lashae hopes her words inspire others to find their own voices and speak their truths unapologetically.

When she is not writing, Lashae enjoys uplifting others, listening to music that moves her soul, and creating moments that matter. She believes poetry is more than art—it's a mirror, a memory, and sometimes, a lifeline.

9 798218 696986